THE MINDFULNESS
JOURNAL FOR KIDS

the MINDFULNESS JOURNAL for KIDS

Guided Writing Prompts
to Help You Stay Calm,
Positive, and Present

Hannah Sherman, LCSW

ROCKRIDGE
PRESS

For general information on our other products and services or to obtain technical support, please contact our Customer Care Department within the United States at (866) 744-2665, or outside the United States at (510) 253-0500.

Rockridge Press publishes its books in a variety of electronic and print formats. Some content that appears in print may not be available in electronic books, and vice versa.

TRADEMARKS: Rockridge Press and the Rockridge Press logo are trademarks or registered trademarks of Callisto Media Inc. and/or its affiliates, in the United States and other countries, and may not be used without written permission. All other trademarks are the property of their respective owners. Rockridge Press is not associated with any product or vendor mentioned in this book.

Interior and Cover Designer: Jami Spittler
Art Producer: Hannah Dickerson
Editor: Sabrina Young and Andrea Leptinsky
Production Editor: Rachel Taenzler

All illustrations used under license from Creative Market, Shutterstock.com and iStock.com. Author photo courtesy of Jacquelyn Potter.

ISBN: Print 978-1-64611-172-5
R0

CONTENTS

YOU CAN'T STOP THE WAVES,

BUT YOU CAN

LEARN HOW TO SURF.

—Jon Kabat-Zinn

This Journal Belongs to:

_____

INTRODUCTION

Welcome to your mindfulness journal! I'm so happy you're here. No matter where you are in this world, or what might be going on in your life, this mindfulness journal offers you a place where you can reflect on your thoughts and feelings and find inspiration and calm.

My name is Hannah and I work at a school where I help kids just like you develop the tools they need to tackle tough situations and difficult emotions. And the best way to do that is through the power of mindfulness! I have worked with kids of all ages (and have used mindfulness myself), and I've seen how mindfulness can help us learn from our experiences and the world around us.

This journal is your opportunity to write about your mindfulness experience with curiosity and compassion. I wish you joy and peace as you set off on your mindfulness journey.

What Is Mindfulness?

Have you ever had a busy mind, when your mind was full of thoughts competing for your attention? Having a busy mind sometimes leads to us getting lost in our thoughts or becoming distracted from what we're doing. When you use mindfulness, you become aware of what is happening right now, inside and outside of your body. This is called *being present*.

Being present teaches you to accept your experiences as they are instead of trying to change them, push them away, or label them as wrong. It means staying tuned in to the present moment instead of fighting it. When you're no longer fighting, you can be kinder to yourself and the people around you.

So, how else can mindfulness help you? It can help you stay calm when you're taking a big test at school. It can help you notice when you feel angry, sad, or frustrated before you *act* angry, sad, or frustrated. It can help you treat your friends, your family, and yourself with care and compassion. It can teach you to let go of your worries and stress, and help you stay calm and focused.

There are many different types of mindfulness activities: meditation, breathing exercises, and journaling. This mindfulness journal will help you explore your experiences and learn more about yourself and the world around you.

Being mindful takes some effort. But the more you do it, the easier it gets.

How to Use This Journal

This journal is meant to be an easy and fun way for you to develop your mindfulness practice. (A practice is an activity or exercise you do again and again so you become better at it.) The journal is filled with writing prompts and reflection questions, mindfulness exercises to try out, and powerful quotes from inspiring people. This is your creative space, where you can write, draw, and color in any way that brings you joy.

The best way to get better at using mindfulness is to practice it every day. Make this journal part of your routine by completing one or two writing prompts or trying an exercise every day. As you complete each page, you will get to know yourself better, develop more self-confidence, and gain awareness about who you are and what makes you unique.

Although this journal is meant to help you learn, grow, and manage tough feelings, know that it is still okay to ask for help when you need it. This journal is not meant to take the place of a therapist or medication if you're really struggling with difficult thoughts and feelings. There is no shame in asking for help. Taking care of yourself is what matters. And journaling is just one tool you can use to take care of yourself.

Are you ready to begin your mindfulness journey? Settle in a comfortable seat, take a deep breath, and let's begin!

YOU ARE HERE

Begin your mindfulness journey by learning how to find peace in the present moment—the moment you're in right now. In the next few pages, you'll learn how to become more aware of the present moment by getting curious about your mind, your body, and the world around you. The prompts and practices in this section will help you discover a few tools to deal with each moment as it comes.

Start your mindfulness journal by setting some intentions. An *intention* is something you plan to do. When you set intentions, you are taking the first step toward making your hopes and dreams come true. Perhaps you want to learn more about yourself, have more self-confidence, or learn ways to stay calm.

Write down your hopes, dreams, and goals for your mindfulness journey.

....

....

....

....

....

....

....

....

....

....

....

When we worry about the past or the future, it can make us feel stressed. Paying attention to the present moment can help us stay calm. Pause here and ask yourself: What is happening *right now*? What do you notice about yourself and the place where you are at this moment?

Be Here Now

Begin this exercise by writing down an affirmation. An *affirmation* is a positive message that you say to yourself, like "I am a good person." What affirmation could help you be more focused on the present moment?

....

....

....

Now, put your affirmation into action. Find a quiet place where you can stand tall like a tree, with your back straight and your arms at your sides. Make sure the palms of your hands are facing forward. Take a deep breath by inhaling through your nose. Then, as you exhale through your mouth, say your affirmation out loud.

Take three deep breaths. Repeat your affirmation each time you exhale.

LIVE TODAY. NOT YESTERDAY.
NOT TOMORROW.
JUST TODAY.
INHABIT YOUR MOMENTS.
DON'T RENT THEM OUT
TO TOMORROW.

—Jerry Spinelli, *Love, Stargirl*

Come to Your Senses

Another way you can use mindfulness is to become aware of what's happening outside of your body. This is called "tuning in to your senses." (Do you remember what the five senses are? They are seeing, hearing, smelling, tasting, and touching.)

Write down three things you see, hear, or feel in this moment.

....

....

....

Look around. What do you see? Are you inside or out-side? Is it sort of dark or is there a lot of light?

I see . . .

....

....

....

....

....

Now, listen. What do you hear? Are the sounds very low or loud?

I hear . . .

....

....

....

....

....

Reach out your hand. What can you touch or feel? Are your feet touching the ground? What do you feel with your feet?

I feel . . .

....

....

....

....

....

Being Mindful of Scent

This exercise will help you tune in to your sense of smell. You're going to sniff a piece of fruit—and you're going to do it mindfully! You'll want to use a piece of fruit that is easy to smell, like a strawberry or an orange.

- Start by holding the piece of fruit in your hand. How does it feel? Is it smooth or rough? Is it hard or soft?

- Hold the piece of fruit up to your nose and inhale slowly. Is the scent strong or do you barely smell it? Does it smell like you thought it would?

- Now, close your eyes and smell the piece of fruit again. Has its smell changed? If you think it has, how has it changed?

- If the fruit has a skin (like an orange or a banana), slowly peel off the skin and smell the piece of fruit for the last time—really take in its scent! How has the smell of the fruit changed now that there's no skin?

- Finally, take a bite of the fruit! Does it taste like it smelled?

Thoughts pass through our minds like water flowing down a river. The thoughts never stop! What thoughts are in your mind at this moment? Are there many thoughts or just a few? Do your thoughts move fast or slow? How many different thoughts can you have?

Write down each thought in your mind and what you notice about it.

....

....

....

....

....

....

....

....

....

....

Our breath is a powerful tool. It tells us how we're feeling, and it can help us calm our bodies when we're feeling upset or stressed.

Pause for a minute and notice how you're breathing right now. Can you hear the sound of your breath? What does it sound like? Where do you feel the breath in your body as you inhale and exhale? What else do you notice?

....

....

....

....

....

....

....

....

....

....

Deep Belly Breaths

Paying attention to your breath can help you stay mindful. This breathing exercise will teach you how to use your breathing to get a feeling of calm.

- Find a comfortable place to sit and close your eyes.

- Put one hand on your belly so that you can feel your body as you breathe.

- Take a deep breath in through your nose. Fill your belly up like a balloon!

- Breathe out slowly through your mouth.

- Notice the sounds as you exhale. Let it all go.

- Take three more deep belly breaths.

- Feel your belly rise as you inhale and fall as you exhale.

When we do things that make us feel calm or happy, we are taking care of ourselves, because we are making ourselves feel better.

What are some things that make you feel relaxed or full of joy? Maybe you like making art, playing with friends, or going for a bike ride. Take a few minutes to care for yourself right now. Create a list of things you can do to feel calm or happy.

....

....

....

....

Now, think about how each of these different activities makes you feel. Describe the feelings you get when you do these activities.

....

....

....

....

....

Musical Meditation

This practice uses music to help you tune in to the present!

Find a quiet place where you won't be disturbed. Take a comfortable seat and spend some time listening to a song that you enjoy.

As you listen, choose one part of the song to pay special attention to. This could be the words, one of the instruments, or the tune. As you listen, notice when your mind wanders away from the song. When it does, gently bring your attention back to the song. Pay attention and continue listening.

When the song is over, notice how you feel. Did the music make you calm or excited? Happy or sad?

The part of the song I listened to was . . .

. . . .

. . . .

The song made me feel . . .

. . . .

. . . .

. . . .

A LITTLE CONSIDERATION,
A LITTLE THOUGHT
FOR OTHERS, MAKES ALL
THE DIFFERENCE.

—A. A. Milne, *Winnie the Pooh*

Where are you right now? Maybe you're in a place that's familiar to you, like your bedroom or a park. Wherever you are, is it a calm and comforting place for you? Describe what you hear, and what you can feel, touch, and smell.

....

....

....

....

....

....

....

....

....

....

....

....

If where you are right now is not calm, then imagine a place that is comforting to you. Where is that place? What might you see there? Write down how that comforting place makes you feel.

....

....

....

....

....

....

....

....

....

....

....

....

Find Your Comforts

When we have feelings like sadness, frustration, and anxiety, being comforted can help. Comfort might feel like a warm hug, taste like your favorite food, or smell like flowers.

Now, go explore a few comforting senses! Describe the places, tastes, smells, and sounds that help you feel comforted.

When I'm in my comforting place, I see . . .

....

....

....

....

When I think of a comforting food, I taste . . .

....

....

....

....

When I think of a comforting scent, I smell . . .

....

....

....

....

When I think of a comforting sound, I hear . . .

....

....

....

....

How do you feel when you're worried or when you can't decide what to do?

....

....

Now, imagine yourself as the hero in your favorite story. Describe your character and what makes you special.

....

....

Now that you're the hero of your story, what would you do if you had a problem to deal with?

....

....

....

....

....

....

AT THE END OF THE DAY,
WE CAN ENDURE
MUCH MORE
THAN WE THINK WE CAN.

—Frida Kahlo

STAYING WITH DIFFICULTIES

Difficult feelings like anger, sadness, anxiety, and jealousy are like rainstorms. They can be unpleasant and feel like they will last forever. But, just like a rainstorm, all difficult feelings eventually pass.

Using mindfulness can help us stay with difficult feelings until the storm passes and the sun shines again. You might wonder, why would we want to stay with a difficult feeling? Because when we notice difficult feelings, we have more control over *them* than they have over *us*.

When we're aware of having these feelings, we can pause and then choose how we want to respond instead of reacting without any thought at all. For example, instead of yelling at your sibling when you're frustrated, you could try taking a deep breath to calm yourself instead.

Being aware of your difficult emotions in the moment you're feeling them can help you respond to them in a healthy way.

Sometimes when we feel angry, anxious, or sad, we try to push those feelings away. But the feelings don't go away—they build up instead. The feelings become like water filling a bucket. And what will happen to that bucket eventually? It will overflow.

This is what happens when our difficult feelings build up—they start to "overflow" into our actions. For example, when anger builds up, it might lead us to yell at someone when we don't mean to.

Check in with your feelings now. Are there any difficult feelings that seem like they might overflow? Name each feeling. What can you do to take care of these feelings before they overflow?

Naming difficult feelings when they happen is another way that we can keep those feelings from taking over. Naming a feeling while we're having it makes us more aware of it. It's present. It's with us. And we no longer need to push it away.

Think about three feelings you've experienced today. Now, use those feelings to finish the sentences below by gently saying to yourself, "It's okay to feel ...."

It's okay to feel . . .

....

....

It's okay to feel . . .

....

....

It's okay to feel . . .

....

....

TRY TO BE
A RAINBOW
IN SOMEONE'S
CLOUD.

—Maya Angelou

Sight Scan

This calming exercise uses the sense of sight to help you focus on the present moment when big feelings take over!

- Find a comfortable place to sit, either in your bedroom or somewhere outside.

- Close your eyes, then take a deep breath.

- Now, open your eyes and scan the space around you. Notice what you see.

- Focus on the details of the objects around you. Notice what you see.

- Look for five different colors.

- End this exercise by coloring in each of the five circles, on the right, with the colors that you see.

I'M NOT AFRAID OF STORMS,
FOR I'M LEARNING
HOW TO SAIL MY SHIP.

—Louisa May Alcott,
Little Women

Being curious about difficult feelings can make it easier to let them be present with us when they happen. Think about a difficult feeling you had today. Maybe it was sadness or frustration. What was it like when you had this feeling? Finish the sentences below.

Today, I felt . . .

....

....

What made me feel this way was . . .

....

....

My body responded to this feeling by . . .

....

....

When I feel like this, my thoughts are . . .

....

....

Having difficult feelings is hard, but you're not alone. Everyone has them. All our feelings—good and bad, pleasant and difficult—are part of what makes us human.

Name three difficult feelings that you have right now. Who do you know who has those feelings, too? If you shared your feelings with someone else, do you think it would help you feel less alone?

Legs up the Wall

For this exercise, grab a pillow and find an area where you can lay down with your back on the floor and your butt up against a bare wall. Make sure there's plenty of space around you.

- Place the pillow under your head so that you're comfortable lying down.

- Gently bring your legs up so that they are resting against the wall. Scoot your butt closer to the wall if you need to.

- Place your hands on your belly.

- Take three deep breaths. Inhale through your nose as you count to three, then exhale through your mouth as you count to three.

- Repeat these three deep breaths three times.

This posture helps send signals to your body to calm down and relax when difficult feelings arise.

Soothing Stress

Think about a time when you felt stressed or anxious.
Maybe you were having trouble with your homework
or you had a fight with your best friend. When we're
stressed or anxious, it's hard to remember to keep our
focus on the present moment! We're busy thinking
about what might happen in the future or what happened in the past.

When we focus on the present moment, the stress we
feel can be reduced. This lets us respond to the stress in
a thoughtful way, instead of just reacting.

List the things that make you feel stressed and all the
activities that make you feel better.

What makes me feel stressed is . . .

....

....

....

....

....

....

....

....

....

....

....

....

What makes me feel better is . . .

....

....

....

....

....

....

....

....

....

Channeling Positivity

Sometimes when we feel sad, angry, or anxious, we start thinking negative thoughts. These negative thoughts can keep us "stuck" in our difficult feelings.

When you catch yourself having a negative thought, try to change the thought by looking at the situation differently. For example, if you get a low score on your science test, instead of thinking "I'm stupid," you can change the thought to "I have trouble in some classes, but I do really well in others."

Looking at the "big picture," and not just one thing, can help you change a negative thought into a positive one.

Write down a negative thought that you have sometimes. Then write down a way to change the thought into a positive one!

A negative thought I have is . . .

....

....

....

....

....

....

....

....

A way to change that thought to a positive one is . . .

....

....

....

....

....

....

....

....

....

....

Sometimes difficult emotions make us feel stuck. We keep thinking about what caused the difficult emotion. Maybe it was a fight with a parent, drama with a friend, or a problem at school. We just can't stop thinking about what happened! And we're stuck with the difficult emotion it made us feel.

What does it feel like to be in that stuck place? What thoughts and feelings do you have when you feel stuck?

....

....

....

....

....

....

....

....

....

....

Find Your Footing

Being mindful of your body can help you find a sense of calm when big feelings come up. For this exercise, you're going to practice finding your footing when you're feeling stuck.

- Find a comfortable seat that lets you sit with your feet flat on the floor.

- Close your eyes. Notice how your feet feel resting on the floor.

- Move your feet from side to side.

- Bring your attention to your left foot.

- Now, bring your attention your right foot.

- Wiggle your toes.

- Slowly bring your attention to each toe, starting with your right pinky toe.

- Let your feet to be still and feel supported by the ground.

Feelings in My Body

Feelings can cause different sensations in your body. Your body might feel tense when you're stressed, and it might feel full of energy when you're happy.

For each sentence in this section, describe how your body feels when you have that emotion.

When I feel sad, my body . . .

....

....

....

....

When I feel angry, my body . . .

....

....

....

....

When I feel jealous, my body . . .

....

....

....

....

When I feel stressed, my body . . .

....

....

....

....

ONLY WHEN OUR CLEVER
BRAIN AND OUR
HUMAN HEART WORK
TOGETHER IN HARMONY
CAN WE ACHIEVE OUR
FULL POTENTIAL.

—Jane Goodall

Difficult feelings, like anger and frustration, can pop up quickly! One way to become aware of these feelings is to notice what your body does when you have these emotions. Do you make fists with your hands when you feel frustrated? Do you frown or shake your head when you feel angry?

   In the space below, draw how your body looks when you feel angry or frustrated.

Use words to describe the feelings in your body.

....

....

....

....

Fists of Frustration

This exercise will teach you a way to let go of anger and frustration in your body.

- Find a comfortable seat, then close your eyes.

- Inhale through your nose and tighten your hands into fists.

- Hold your breath for a count of three while you squeeze your fists.

- Slowly exhale through your mouth as you open your hands. As you let your hands relax, imagine you are letting go of all your feelings of anger and frustration.

- Repeat this exercise three times.

When we have difficult feelings, saying kind words to ourselves can help us feel comforted and supported. For example, you might say to yourself, "Everyone feels sad sometimes. It's okay to feel that way."

Can you think of some kind words you can say to yourself when you're feeling sad or hurt? Write a letter to yourself as if you were your best friend. Include kind words of support. Read this letter for comfort the next time you feel sad or hurt.

....

....

....

....

....

....

....

....

Color Your Rainbow

You've done a lot of work on how to deal with difficult feelings. It's time to get out some crayons or pencils and draw!

Close your eyes and think of your favorite colors. Write down the names of the colors here.

Now, use these colors to draw your "relaxation rainbow." As you draw, keep your focus on the page. Notice how your hand feels as it moves across the paper. If your mind drifts to thoughts of something else, gently bring it back to your drawing.

BEING GRATEFUL

Gratitude means being thankful for the things that you appreciate in your life. Showing gratitude—in other words, being grateful—can help you stay positive and feel a sense of joy!

Growing Gratitude

Instead of feeling like we need or want something else to make us happy, gratitude helps us be thankful for what we already have. We can be grateful for the people in our life, the experiences we've had, and the parts of ourselves that make us who we are!

Creating a gratitude practice is a powerful way to boost your mood. For example, if you find yourself upset after losing a game, gratitude will teach you to appreciate the fun of playing the game, no matter what the end result is.

Use the following prompts to create a list of all the people, places, and things that bring you happiness and joy.

I'm grateful for [person] because . . .

....

....

....

....

....

I'm grateful to be in or go to [place] because it makes me feel . . .

....

....

....

....

....

I'm grateful for these things about myself because they make me feel . . .

....

....

....

....

....

Try to remember moments of joy so you can stay positive and not get stuck being negative.

What brought you joy this week? It might be something that happened at school or home. Maybe it happened when you were alone, or maybe it happened when you were with the people you love. Think about what you saw, heard, smelled, or felt during that moment of joy.

Now, describe that experience. Include as many details as possible.

Gratitude Walk

One great way to get into a positive mood is to go on a gratitude walk!

Take a walk outside so that you can appreciate your surroundings. Notice the smell of flowers or trees. Breathe in the fresh air. What else can you see, hear, smell, or touch?

In the space below, draw three things that you noticed during your walk.

I AM CONTENT IN KNOWING
I AM AS BRAVE
AS ANY BEAST THAT EVER
LIVED, IF NOT BRAVER.

—L. Frank Baum,
The Wonderful Wizard of Oz

Sometimes we have thoughts about ourselves that are not nice at all. We may judge ourselves harshly and criticize ourselves unfairly.

For instance, say you got a low grade on a math test. You might think to yourself, "I'm so stupid!" This harsh judgment comes from the critic inside of you. Even though the thought isn't true, it can be hard not to believe it.

To quiet the critic inside of you, try to come up with some kind and encouraging responses to those judgmental thoughts. If that math test didn't go well, you can say, "It's okay that this happened. Nobody's perfect. Everyone makes mistakes. I can try again next time!"

Write down a few kind and encouraging responses to the critic inside of you. Pay special attention to the tone of your responses and the words you might use.

Showing Yourself Kindness

This powerful exercise is a loving-kindness practice that you can use when the critic inside of you gets too loud. A loving-kindness practice focuses on being gentle and considerate toward yourself and others.

- Find a quiet and comfortable place to sit.

- Place your hands on your heart and close your eyes.

- Notice your breath. Notice how it feels in your body as you breathe in and out.

- As you breathe, gently say to yourself, "I am loved."

- Repeat these words three times.

What feelings, colors, or sensations did you become aware of when you said these loving words to yourself?

....

....

....

....

Reflecting on what makes you special and unique can improve your self-esteem (how you think about yourself)!

Close your eyes and imagine that you are looking in a mirror. Notice how it feels to see your reflection in the mirror. What do you see that makes you unique? Write down some positive words to describe who you are.

....

....

....

....

....

....

....

....

....

What makes you feel safe? Maybe it's a close friendship, a comforting place, or a special song. Think about all the things, big and small, that give you this feeling. Write down at least three things that make you feel safe.

....

....

....

....

....

....

....

....

....

Think about someone you care about very much. It might be a family member, a teacher, or a good friend. Why do you care about this person so much? Think about how they make you feel and why you are grateful for this relationship.

Write some kind wishes that you can share with this person. For example, you might say, "May you be happy," or, "I hope your dreams come true!" Notice how it feels to write down these wishes.

....

....

....

....

....

....

....

....

KINDNESS
CAN ONLY BE REPAID
WITH KINDNESS.

—Malala Yousafzai

Write a Gratitude Letter

Write a gratitude letter to someone in your life that you would like to thank or show your appreciation. This could be a friend, a family member, or a teacher—whoever you want!

   In the letter, thank this person, and include lots of details about what you appreciate about them and why. If you want to, you can share this letter with them.

Dear ....,

....

....

....

....

....

....

You probably know what it feels like to be angry or upset. But what does it mean to feel calm and balanced? Some people feel calm and balanced when they relax their body, focus their mind on a task, or just breathe slowly in and out.

Try doing each of these actions yourself: relax your body, focus your mind, and breathe slowly. How do your body and mind feel now? Do they feel calm and balanced? Write down how you feel and what helped you feel that way.

....

....

....

Next, think about what other things help you feel calm and balanced. Maybe drawing or making art helps you feel focused. Maybe going for a walk makes your body relax. List some of your favorite activities that help you feel calm and balanced.

....

....

....

Calming Breath

Did you know that when we control our breathing, we send signals to our body to calm down? How cool is that! Let's practice taking a calm breath.

- Find a quiet place where you can stand up with your arms at your sides.

- Take a deep breath in through your nose.

- As you breathe in, raise your arms above your head and touch your palms together.

- As your palms touch, softly say to yourself, "I am calm."

- Exhale through your nose and bring your arms back down to your sides.

- Do this four more times.

Kindness helps us feel positive emotions. What are some ways you've shown kindness to someone, or received kindness? Write about those experiences below.

....

....

....

There are many different ways to be kind to yourself and the people around you. Write down three ways you have been kind to yourself.

....

....

....

Now, list three ways you have been kind to others.

....

....

....

Can you think of some other acts of kindness you could try?

Some acts of kindness I can take toward others are . . .

....

....

....

....

....

Some acts of kindness I can take toward myself are . . .

....

....

....

....

....

WE CARRY WITH US,
AS HUMAN BEINGS,
NOT JUST THE CAPACITY
TO BE KIND,
BUT THE VERY CHOICE
OF KINDNESS.

—R. J. Palacio, *Wonder*

Think about yourself one year ago. Where were you? What were you doing? What images come into your mind when you think about your past self? Write down what your life was like one year ago today.

....

....

....

Now, think about the challenges you have overcome during the past year. Perhaps you had a fight with a friend or a family member, or struggled with an assignment at school. How you were able to deal with these issues and obstacles? How did these experiences help you learn and grow?

....

....

....

....

....

Mantra Magic

Did you know that you have the power to create a sense of joy and peace inside of you? You can do this by coming up with your own mantra. A *mantra* is a positive word, or several words, that you repeat to yourself to help you stay mindful. Your mantra might be a reminder of something important, like "I am safe," "My feelings matter," or "I belong."

Create your own mindfulness mantras! Use these prompts to come up with three different mantras that you can say to yourself to bring a sense of peace. Use colors, draw pictures, or add shapes to turn your mantra into a joyful design that's uniquely yours.

I am . . .

I have . . .

....

....

....

....

....

I try . . .

....

....

....

....

....

Staying Mindful

You've arrived at the end of your journal! But the end of your journal does *not* mean this is the end of your mindfulness journey. Think about how you can use the activities and exercises in this journal to make mindfulness part of your day, every day.

Go ahead and write down one mindfulness practice that you can do during each part of the day.

In the morning, I can use this practice to stay positive.

....

....

....

....

....

....

....

....

At school, I can use this practice to keep my calm.

....

....

....

....

....

....

At night, I can use this practice to feel grateful.

....

....

....

....

....

....

My Mindfulness Journey

This journal is only the first step in your mindfulness journey. Take a moment to think about where your journey began and what you experienced along the way.

What were your feelings when you wrote in this journal?

....

....

....

Which questions were hard to answer?

....

....

....

Which mindfulness exercises helped the most? Why?

....

....

....

Which exercises will you keep using?

....

....

....

Have you changed as a person since you started this mindfulness journal? If so, how?

....

....

....

Feel gratitude for all of these experiences and be proud of all the work you've done!

Yoga and Mindfulness Card Decks

Yoga & Mindfulness Practices for Children or Teens
by Little Flower Yoga

These cards are a perfect way to use mindfulness practices and yoga either at home or on the go. They include many different yoga, meditation, and breathing activities.

Yoga Pretzels: 50 Fun Yoga Activities for Kids and Grownups *by Tara Guber and Leah Kalish*

These cards are a great way to do mindfulness practices through yoga movement. They include ideas for different mindful movements and breathing practices.

Apps

Headspace for Kids

Headspace.com/meditation/kids

You can use this app by downloading it on a phone or tablet (you might need your parents' help!) for fun mindfulness videos and guided meditation practices.

Stop, Breathe & Think Kids

StopBreatheThink.com/kids

This app is made for kids just like you, and it suggests specific mindfulness practices based on how you're feeling. It is so cool!

Books

Alphabreaths: The ABCs of Mindful Breathing
by Christopher Willard and Daniel Rechtschaffen

This illustrated book offers a playful and fun guide to the power of the breath while introducing the basics of mindful breathing.

I Am Human: A Book of Empathy *by Susan Verde*

This beautiful book celebrates the power of empathy and compassion for all parts of yourself and others.

The Mindfulness Coloring Book *by Emma Farrarons*

This book allows you to do mindfulness practices through making art and mindful coloring, two fun ways to find your focus and calm your body.

This Moment Is Your Life (And So Is This One)
by Mariam Gates

This colorful book helps explain the basics of mindfulness and gives you some additional ideas for how to do mindfulness practices on your own.

ABOUT THE AUTHOR

 **Hannah Sherman, LCSW,** is a Brooklyn-based licensed clinical social worker and mindfulness educator. As both a school social worker and a private practice psychotherapist, she supports children, adolescents, and adults in their journey toward healing and growth.

As a children's yoga and mindfulness teacher, she works to help young people use their bodies and minds as tools to navigate their own experiences of the world with curiosity and compassion. Having always honored a holistic lens toward well-being, she is deeply passionate about supporting children in establishing a positive connection to their bodies and feeling empowered by their minds.

She offers education-based and skill-building professional development workshops to helping professionals, including educators and mental health practitioners. She has developed and implemented mindfulness-based programs and curriculum for New York City–based schools. She also provides coaching to caregivers who are interested in bringing mindfulness to their parenting practices.

To learn more about her approach and offerings, visit HannahSherman.com and follow her on Instagram at @HannahShermanTherapy.